# Clarity or Death!

JEFFREY WAINWRIGHT was born in Stoke-on-Trent in 1944 and was educated locally and at the University of Leeds. He has taught at the University of Wales, Long Island University in Brooklyn and for many years at the Manchester Metropolitan University where he was Professor of English until 2008. He is married to Judith Wainwright with whom he has two grown-up children. They live in Manchester and spend some parts of the year in Italy.

Jeffrey Wainwright has written many articles and reviews on poetry and two books of criticism, *Poetry the Basics* (2004) and *Acceptable Words: Essays on the Poetry of Geoffrey Hill* (2005), and has translated plays by Péguy, Corneille, Claudel and Koltès for radio and stage.

JEFFREY WAINWRIGHT

# *Clarity or Death!*

CARCANET

First published in Great Britain in 2008 by
Carcanet Press Limited
Alliance House
Cross Street
Manchester M2 7AQ

A CIP catalogue record for this book is available from the British Library
ISBN 978 1 85754 912 6

The publisher acknowledges financial assistance from Arts Council England

Typeset by XL Publishing Services, Tiverton
Printed and bound in England by SRP Ltd, Exeter

For Judith

*I wish to God that I were more intelligent and everything would finally become clear to me – or else that I didn't live much longer!*

LUDWIG WITTGENSTEIN

*The progression of a painter's work, as it travels in time from point to point, will be towards clarity.*

MARK ROTHKO

# Contents

# The coffee stain

the coffee stain     I'll call it
   on your hip

the many washes of a spill
upon a tablecloth might produce
   just that shade and littoral

but haven't    so far as I am aware


expect by now a love poem
(whosoever might expect)

but what I am saying is not
to do with longing –
the ball of my finger across your nipple
and what would be the lightest touch there –

but with whatever is like and like
within  *blotch  dab  patch*
and is necessary to think of
and beautiful and
like the loveliness of conjunctions
is nowhere

whereas on your hip is one shade and littoral

*we may be able to reduce the number of different things*

i

Here on my little river-beach with Feynman
(he who professes the nose of a spaniel)
I practise the learned thought of how the local heron
will feel the same current in air as in water,
that this flow slips by the delta-wing,
rips the tide round Sark,
braces the fox as he sets
his mask for home,
and that all these can be understood together,
drawn in lines that themselves
bear nothing, move nothing,
yet, with just the faintest nudge for variables,
display the laws that bring the log ashore
like a heavy man.

## ii

It's foreign ground, the sand beneath the fox's foot,
river-borne to the beach by his sloping wood,
and he shakes it from him as he climbs back
into dry shadow and leaf-ground.
This outcrop under his paw could,
in some grindings, also be sand.
In a separate action,
rising with the moon,
the heron lifts
and folds itself back.
Moon, gritstone, sand.

## iii

Rule: there is no cagoule makes no noise.
But before that, much before our yap
and the dogs skidding in the leaves,
with, at most, the push of a breath
a hundred yards before
we have the heron's attention.

It's like a whisper into a dish
collected and conveyed,
like the bang on a can,
the scratch orchestra,
four minutes and whatever
of any sound,
and resolves with them
to a known line
which is in turn like the light wave,
a pond stirring, a hot wire,
the barchans of Turkestan,
the medanos of Peru,
and  – we are bound to think this way –
fibrillation, quivering in the heart –
She used to say, *I can sit here*
*and hear it pounding.*

## iv

Grace Crowley learned in Paris
(*ville d'art*)
to insist on the abstract elements

i.e. line, shape, and colour

i.e. (as I understand it)
what is 'inside' the 'given' space

'given' being a jug, a jar,
a tree, a mountain top

'inside' not cherries, *confiture* or leaf-vein,
and not the label, not the finger-post,
no matter how elegant the letter-form,
especially not the net weights in the glass

just volume:
how much is not
what is around it

and the lines
that mean this

soon less than lines

some shading

her ghost gum wore silver and the spinifex wore grey

## V

to see enough in a few bottles vases and jars,
and to be so compelled says:
here must be the forms
beyond their instances –

and she is in a rage to paint
what she does not see –
from the wilds of the mind
air and light undefiled
so that the bottles vases jars,
though not inimical,
could be swept from the shelf
for they exist otherwise –

only
implying
other
bottles
vases
jars
even
every
one
possible

*Classically*, this moment before the fox
ceases his assizing stare and disappears,
and the heron flaps diagonally to the opposite bank,
and I stop to try to arrest them, is *B*,
a 'point in time', the same in which
the moons of Jupiter, once thought unpunctual
but now recognised as early or late only according to
how near or far from us they are,
send us some particular light;
in which Sirius, borne in on itself
still signals outward; in which … (I could go on).
And *all* are arrived together from *A*,
that is point *A*, the starting point,
and must, by every bearing of the magi,
aligned with every known velocity
and thus made law,
have arrived here in just this order.
Although, *unclassically*, this has always been only
a possibility for there were many paths from *A*,
and few or none would have happened through
this *B* where the fox flickers into a darkness
that would be strange elsewhere,
full of air and built of shadow by just one sun,
held in all its places between sedate gravity
and wild escape,
and with all our fellow elementary dust still arriving
at *C*, which is again hospitable,
even if now cooling differently.

### the starting state of the universe must have been very highly ordered

and even now, with fifteen billion years elusive cooling –
this slow frustration of the boilermaker's art –
the vixen does not find herself with eggs,
the heron need not peck blood to feed her cubs,
once more the comet meets its ETA
and camper-vans assemble for the great eclipse.

Yes, there is *the stealth, the violence, cunning of the sea,*
as there is junkyard DNA, and Poe's odd conchology,
but we that know we nothing were so long,
– *beneath the dust did in a chaos lie* –
and are of a mind to feel the quantum shudder
need not be afeard: the particles do body-pop
and jostle in our sight, but still heed
their codes and nice formations,
and will reorganise tomorrow as we die.

### *the universe is like a pool that has had a stone thrown into it*

And like a high black tarn resuming itself
the ripples would pass away,
land and sky swim together,
that man who by the red dot of his jerkin
can just be seen heaving a heavy cask aboard
will be washed into the land, the land
into the brown sea, into the sky
which might till lately have been likened
to sacking purged of every shade and stain,
every snagged thread and lump-knot,
but now removes itself and every likening,
even the ideas of stitch and knot,
dissolved with the stars into

default                          the restitution of all things
                    when we speak of peace

*'Then is the seriousness of life done away with,' said B.*

*'I am going to rejoin the Real,' said A.*

*all the ordered forms of energy in the universe would*
*ultimately find themselves degraded*

The effort of the heronry and earth
arrests disorder, at least that of the random twig
snapped out of its purposeful economy:
thus is its messed-up, evaporating energy
re-applied and the tidy nest
postpones          the inchoate –
       heaven and earth passed away
imagined as buzz        drone        background

But that is coming, though it will not come,
for there can be no point of arrival
even though the cost borne by the nest
in the burn of starch and sugar
is given off without recapture.
It seems a heel-and-toe business,
and they raise their young. But at length
the housekeeping goes awry, the heronry
is deserted, the ground unlit, untenable,
and always the measurable tendency is outward –
a feather lost and blowing away,
every star passing to the same consistency –
a *purity* it might be called in some quarters.

# Oh! Oh!

Oh! (and Oh!) this pretending to the void!
this always being sweet
on the pebble-dashed nebulae,
this peddling of (and into) the sumptuous blue,
the razor-slash – *uh! uh!* – struck through
into blackness,
beyond, beyond,
always the space beyond
as though there is a nothing we can know
that will not cool, carbonise
at least into a dot, a splotch, a word,
not always some thing,
be it so indefinite, so infinite
as balance upon a beam, or on a wire across the
– *ahem* – where the artiste takes his tea

everywhere else is not mystery it is death

### *there may be symmetrical universes but they are not ours*

You always knew sir, didn't you,
that what we see and draw cannot exist?
However wide our local heavens can become,
no conjunction and no crystal, however deep,
will give us a circle unbubbled at its edge,
a triangle in precise equipoise,
an any-hedron that is not anyhow,
even fleetingly, because
though *symmetries break reluctantly*,
they break, ours break certainly,
and thus the measuring begins,
even if we were barely shuddering here,
and we are not.
But please still see them sir.

# a point is never alone

In Mr Cooksey's Technical Drawing class dots would never do.
Joining up two soft-pencil puddles of lead
will get you from where to where?
And if your line is a stubby 5B thick,
a dimension *we* can see never mind dust-mites with their wagon-trains,
where has it arrived?
Draw like that and your tea-tray will be wonky,
your screw-thread strip itself,
your piston grate in your cylinder. *Snigger snigger*.

So, first, the perfection, over weeks in the Woodwork Shop,
of the sandpaper block.
Now a good 4H could be shaded fine enough
to make a hairline cross,
and the narrowest line could join them,
just as in geometry, where your pencil should also be sharp –
*Sharp, boy, sharp as the point of your compasses* –
and places that have no parts or magnitude –
that do not exist –
will arrive at your desk here on the top corridor
as squares, triangles, parallelograms,
and, between these non-existent points,
we get a table-lamp we can take home.

## ii

but there are still hikers afoot
across the finest line:
on and on, (or down and down)
the point descends,
a sea-stack of the hardest lead,
within it the same magnitudes
as of the universe to Earth,
Earth to atom, nucleus to whatever,
are vibrating there and on to wherever gravity
is seeping to, to whatever is happening to time

– When are we stopping sir?
Please sir, Mr Cooksey, we cannot believe in nothing.

### iii

*musicians wrestle everywhere*
as do the numberers, their kith and kin,
who starting, perforce, from here,
would rise and bring the nearby wanderers
every shovelful of dust,
every passing flare of hydrogen
into a reckoning
so they can rock together,
swing to the same algorithm:
the falling almond
and the furthest curvature.

And it will be true:
the Form of things,
and most beautiful because
it is its indifferent self,
recognised only in our imaginings

knows nothing

but in our staunch imaginings

## iv

Why did I choose almonds as an image
in this advocacy?
Certainly because I have this tree to sit beneath,
its scatterings are many though not a myriad –
they will not do, for instance, for stars.
Custom of poem and the summer's chance
bring the almonds into work.
You could say thus was it written,
but also that the almonds that are not stars
fall randomly on to this page as on the grass.
The thought of almonds and the thought of stars,
or the thought of samphire cut and out for sale,
the collarless recluse with his cellar junk and firewood,
the man with the ear-scar in the Services –
Star and almond and their various velocities,
yes, well, their tandem will be seen,
but then the samphire, and the men,
which could be waves alone and never caught upon the gel?
*Collar, cellar* – ok ok
that's a function – let's now extrapolate
the shifty universe of albumen and stars.

# by categories do we maister [master] the world

we always think that we are looking on looking in

that it is in us to see

that it is the long-nosed mouse underground
gobbling the artichoke roots
that the diamondback's a heat-seeker
that we can read the broken sand
revealed by dawn
the scutter-marks and fine-drilling
all for food and danger

we always think we are looking on looking in

sand   scutter   snake   snout-mouse
if we speak them they will be –
and made ours by arrangement

the bones rattled cunningly in a cup
scutter across the baize till time runs out
and 'warming' will work for any creature
of the genus ectotherm (though it must be tested)

and skink shall beget skink unto the last generation


yet we are made lonely by our categories
for nothing else owns them

# facts: I bounce my ball

*I bounce my ball against my stone*
*I bounce my ball against my stone*

for you this wall is real, a fact,
and 'brute' in that for all your powers
you cannot pass through it,
and that its stones, like its cousins in the gorge below,
need no requirement of yours to be

the water there also is 'brute': it cut the gorge
and could drown you, even though
the dam now holds it in the concept 'lake',
though I would not call that 'institutional' exactly,
not like a coin from the excavation
which will fall helplessly through every slot
but still belongs to 'money', and you know
how real that is, the part it has in digging the clay,
logging the forest, firing the kiln,
trading the ware downstream,
the dishes, the bowls, the amphorae
*for* oil *for* wine *for* dinner
and how all conurbations need
customs and laws which will also be brutal
but only exist because you say so
for even when engraved a law is not a stone

*I bounce my ball against my stone*
*I bounce my ball against my stone*
*I bounce my ball against my stone*

# we so love the laws

we will rush into crazy houses
into the pill that makes us small
shriek at mirrors that draw us out like gum
or smear us across the glass
knowing it's all four-square really
your Harlech Castle your Tower of London
load-bearing up to the attic the skylight the stars
some of which we know will be where we find them

or they might, like this world does, say:
*You know I am here*, but then shuffle
so 3 will not follow 2
the lift might go in any direction
the turn-right to the shops
will not be the same turn-up tomorrow

so I settle on tapping the same tooth for hours
look at one horseman in the carpet forever
I hear this noise *uv uv uv uv* but there's nothing in it
what is this at my skin?

## against those who refuse definitions

Let us set foot aboard the trireme and I will say
it is a man, you will say it is a wall
while the captain holds fast to his oar.
Or – no.  So, to refer to recent cases, let us simplify
and say a heron and a river are the same thing
and that therefore you can step into the same fox twice,
whether it be that one this morning fleeing from the bins,
this one in the knitting pattern or even that Basil Brush,
although he pretends to a name all his own.
Thus undefined let's say they and we
are all things together, just as the old heron
when at last it stumbles and drowns
is obviously the river, just as we are so much water,
just as the trireme will have its wooden walls
as Nelson did 'gainst Reynard and his crafty crew.
The captain tries to hold fast but we yaw.

Next week we will come on to galley-slaves.

*what need we know of the workings of Nature in order to*
*appreciate how consciousness may be a part of it?*

there will most likely be a rule

but

I do not think an earthquake thinks
as I think,
nor the coral, nor the wasp's nest

for instance I think I can decide
whether to dive today: yes or no
it feels simple enough
and started only this morning –
it does not feel as though a billion steps
have come to this:
I will / I will not
flop off the stern today

then suppose otherwise: suppose I've burnt my foot
and this black tissuey skin is shredding
by rule – not one that 'decreed'
I would burn my foot today,
but one that said
the cells will fall this way
and this way shares a property
with the growth of coral and the wasp's nest
and even with the shuffling of plates
or dominoes?

*faith in reason is the trust that the ultimate natures of things lie together in a harmony which excludes mere arbitrariness*

the periodic tiling of the wasp's nest, or coral

but then a fox under the breakfast table

and faith in the order of things
takes a knock,
               though it was,
as you would expect, running for its life
at the time so there will be a thus and thus

does this mean that as I descend the page
the arbitrary must always elude me,
that however much I strive to be undeliberate,
cut paste and randomise or go automatic
out of dreams or dominoes,
or the thoughtless ingenuity embodied
in the mouse, the arrival of Kirkland's
Warbler here, or August as Kintore,
though yet to be understood by you
could be, should you be interested enough?

What would really count?
Can I who's seen my Dad take the coal-hammer
to treacle-toffee and a Christmas nut
act words no explanatory power on earth could crack?

Stop it now.   We cannot have faith
in the arbitrary, though some profess it,
and are happy that freedom must equal chance.
Are they more comforted than those of us
who long for it all to *lie together*?

# The abstraction of number is beautiful

Take *five*: drums, bass, rhythm, lead and vocals
in a pub in Ashton-under-Lyne,
or Newcastle-under-Lyme,
Hell's Kitchen, a garage in Texas,
a dark park in Dortmund;
Matthews McIlroy Mortensen Mudie Mitchell,
though they can never have played together –
would that they had (only for Stoke though);
Napoleon's victories: Austerlitz, Eylau, Jena,
Wagram, Borodino – *Borodino? Not so fast*,
says Tolstoy: *... cloudlets of smoke ...*
*historical science in its endeavour*
*to draw nearer to truth ... the smell*
*of saltpetre and blood ...*
Gimme five, 'I'll give it foive', top five, first five,
five-star, Five-live, fish alive, more than, less than,
(trochaic five), best of five, starting five: Frazier, Bradley,
Barnett, DeBusschere and Reed – (iambic five? not quite)
but they did play together, and didn't they play Terry?
and I see you in a dream on 5th above Fifth
your jump shot fading to the basket ...
five for the symbols at your door,
brag, stud, par, petals, loaves, parts of the body.

Here – independent of all *things* –
is the use, wonder and beauty of what we cannot see.

### *...and with the Indian figures 987654321 and zephira all calculations are democratically possible*

i

We could *by algorisme tell the gravell of the sea*,
though would such a use count among its treasures?
Written in the sand, the tens and units would stretch along the shore,
but its few strokes still economise on abacists.
Without *zefira* there was nothing,
no way of writing nothing;
with it every distance,
every credit, every debt,
and how the universe bends round itself:
*the decrees of physics are the decrees of fate.*

## ii

That so much and so many could be hidden
in these ciphers, that is the mystery the Saracens
have brought us in *sifr*, *zefira*,
a breath of the west wind,
yet less even than that;
the bundled sticks of stars, the gravel sets:
*zero*, *shûnya*, empty hands, nothing

### iii   *a real sum is a sum of real people*

But I can catch a chill, an *algory* indeed,
as I glimpse something fearful in ciphering,
what those might have meant who called it
*easy Satanism*: the million dead
so easily summ'd up:
*neither one nor two nor three*
*but a poor cipher.*
We can be who we are
but *other men stande for no more than Cypheres*
*in Algorisme* – they are the versatile sand-wave
and do not stand.

*the wall that separates the living from one another*
*is no less opaque than the wall that separates*
*the living from the dead*

After a couple we wave and say goodnight to S,
half-under the porch, one shoulder
of his Oxfam zoot-suit
black with rain, his too-small baseball cap
pushed up on hair you'd think
was treated daily with cement-dust,
the can in his hand,
and he says *G'night*, as though
we could see who is standing there,
as though he could walk through the door
of The Oak without needing to be
bold as brass, as though there are no
walls of brass between him and the barmaid
and the horseshoe of drinkers debating
how you run cars on cooking-oil.

Does he more easily walk through walls
with a pack-mule,
and cross the lobby unmolested,
and find his Gran, or whoever it is
he may want to see, up in her room
with everything tidy and smoothing out
her best dress to welcome him?

# Mere Bagatelle

*... sometimes, out of the corner of an eye, 'at the moment which is not action or inaction', one can glimpse the true scientific vision: austere, tragic, alienated and supremely beautiful. A world that isn't for anything, a world that is just there.*

Jerry Fodor

# 1

the usual thing would be
to look up at night –
there, there, there it is!
or, more often now,
to squirrel into the lawn –
there, there, there it is!
somewhere under the nail

must it still have names?

no, leave that aside –
there is this idea
of its beauty

## 2

the stars are nearly perfect
(for this)
they have a sort of light –
bare-faced metallic,
as seen in dark, grey-brown sand –
and their famous twinkling
is like a blind smile
that is ideal
for their ignorance

even if they are caught up
in what admits,
in what permits us

## 3

but that we are permitted
does not mean
that anything is counted,
still less provided for

this fact can be called 'austere'
as in 'an austere regime'
or 'that was an austere look
she gave me'

# 4

so what could be the
paragons by which
to see ourselves?

the gods nagged
and are gone –
discontinued the huffers-puffers,
randy, watery, windy, owl-eyed,
blood-drenched interferers,
presidents of rocks, springs,
boggart and quarry-holes

 (see how easy this
embellishing is?)

though even with just the One,
who has no body,
parts, or passions,
a tossed date-stone
puts out an eye
and starts some tale running

# 5

(*though,* like *so nevertheless thus*
*therefore sometimes however but* –
is going, loosely speaking,
to be a problem here throughout;
along with *one can,*
and especially *we*
as in *we* do [smell the mint]
– *who* does? me and Lindsay Lohan? –
*we think* [if lintily];
*but* I do *know* –
we do know this don't we? –
that I AM WRITING A POEM
[some of us like to be reminded
of this at regular intervals:
it makes us feel justified somehow
it seems; but more do not
and think conjunctions
adverbs prepositions
are such presumptuous
abstracted devils –
they want to smell the mint!]
*but*, even here, in poem,
we are not saved
from cogitating –
and anyway if you think on things,
Lucretius said,
it'll learn you to relax,
and Virgil,
he found verses appropriate
to advise on sheep-dip)

## 6

there is a shoot of stones
or swallows,
the fringe–drops
of a storm

there is number
or there is not

than that there is,
nothing is more surprising
in Nature

than that we find it anyway
nothing is more surprising
in Nature

(this has been noted more than once)

but, either way,
are they, the figures,
austere enough?

## 8

when Mr Preece taught me to count,
each numeral stood on the clock
as golden and as palpable
as he in his railways wais'cot
with its 6 crested buttons,
or as the troughs
in next door's greenhouse
the handfuls of hard tomatoes
the weights and scales
the raised iron blisters
of av'rdupoise

no, never austere enough

## 9

since no two tomatoes
on the scale,
no two globes we know
are the same,
is it they,
or the idea of the sphere
that is beautiful
if we do just catch sight
of our Creation?

## 10

see also John Ruskin's drawing-lessons:

*'set yourself steadily to conquer that round stone,
and you have won the battle. Look your stone
antagonist boldly in the face.'*

## 11

most of what is beautiful
cannot be so –
we say swallows
diving and cutting
are beautiful
then recognise
their labour
in an early dusk;
the silk-worm's spinning,
the bat-hawk's streaming upwards
are hard yakka,
desperate even

and all our stories
are desperate:
narrow escapes
and passing saints,
how to recuperate
the unhappiness of girls,
or taste their sorrow

perhaps it must be
what is most
inanimate:
it is Rafaello's line,
twenty centimetres
over the brow
to the throat
that makes
his madonna care
but without what we hope for
of maternal love –
take away the child,
what happens
to the line?
is it then
a scratch on a wall
where a truck reversed?
human art
always winks at us

like this,
teases like
an irregular tapping
quite distant
and out of sight

so what, among
the mathematics
where we live, is
unaffected,
as far from ladies' slippers
as can be?
certainly
it must stand
without us:
in balance
and with nothing
remaindered

but why do we wish that?
why, when we like the line
that seems beyond us,
but is not?

## 12

there are things we used to call blessèd
meaning damned:
bootlaces, wallpapering,
knitting, plug-wires,
anything that can get
into a robble

blessèd is the way we are here
as the world surrenders
such of its simplicities as gravity
and the jigger for red hair
etcetera etcetera
but goes on and comes back for more

## 13

such words are still with us,
mostly for talking to those
who cannot hear or cannot reply
or who are truly busy

blessèd now are the micro-explainers
the improvers of sutures

the peacemakers obviously
where they can be found

of course it's not stupid
to talk to no effect

## 14

meanwhile
on they go,
the *vast Rondures,*
swimming past Neptune,

and the base pairs
and the conserved sequences
and our surprising cousin yeast,
copying itself, varying, selecting
and thus going on,
and I will call him cousin
not just to humble us,
but because he must be found a place
in the saga

## 15

but again,
what would the saga be
in which we do
meet ourselves?

it should be a story
of good heart:
*of cousinhood or uncleship –*
let me listen, let me
*for a brief while*
*lay down*
*this solitary bachelorship*
*of mine*

that should be the lyrics
book and score

# 16

if it is not,
if that cannot be assured to us ...

who could bear a story
where her imprisonment
was never at an end
where both were eaten
by every dragon
where we are the giant's
footfall
and feel nothing
but his rage?

each of these would be
a story that returns us nothing,
as where the souls
are harried and fly
but never move

# 17

this clay that stands in
for the human head
is true

though it does not cry
it is tugged up
to the side

and it is lettered:
basic Latin, Arabic–
extended, Hebrew,
Cyrillic, Greek –
pressed, incised,
ledged into
scabbed on to the clay
by now with every bit taken

it must want
to be read

# 18

perhaps he is stamped
with broken names,
one among them his own,
and this is his torment –
how many names
can a man bear?
each lost,
mislaid,

*vous avez perdu l'homme*
*il faudra le retrouver*
*ce ne sera pas facile*

you (?) have lost man,
he must be found again,
it will not be easy to do

## 19

time then for the man
at least as perfect
as the stars,
or at least as sheer,
'bare-faced metallic',
and with a modern purity

he will be unwritten

he will carry nothing
on or about him

as he progresses,
as he lifts each foot,
the step will be erased

he will need nothing
to care for

he can live here

he will just be here

## 20

taking the sun apart
has proved the easier
the advice was clear
and has been heeded:
wait and watch,
let the universe
with all its
unnamed stars
and coloured sands and soils
think us out
and then bow
as the cards are time-lapsed
across the palm
elegantly,
and certainly

– tired anyway
of the great logics
embowelled
in us

## 21

though what is in us
was once without us,
'out there' until
whipped up from dust
till we are like we are now,
djinns careering,
small clouds
forming and reforming,
adjusting stars,
erecting our systems
of stones and flowers
high and low,
racing to the ship pursued,
struggling
with our law-making
like bathers
with their clothes,
and with all the styles
of love:
vast exaltation,
and the children our gift
locked in the car
and asphyxiated
along with him or her

# 22

*after Alberto Burri*


if I see the universe
as a piece
of sacking
half a metre square
used and re-used
snagged
knotted
jabbed with red paint
an oil-drip
some stencilling
and that's all,
I am in error

in the way that I am
unnatural though,
that is what I see

# 23

words, and other
of our imaginings –
lines, sounds –
are the confounding
of Nature –

enough already,
cries She,
of Jairus' daughter (12)
and the combing out
of hell,
or even Homer
Simpson squeezed
through a worm-hole
and escaped to tell

these are uneven and
unfinished doings,
grass cuttings,
mere bagatelle

how little creates
it seems:
a dot, a fast line,
and with the right smudge
the painter can get
a window certainly,
a distant deckchair,
another and another one,
and then the naked board
can serve untouched
as a beach for the people
who are there too,
one hopping
into trousers,
another dozing
with a book

the pier-lights
are coming on,
greasepaint
cane and fedora
a soft-shoe
a sad face,
and it's all purple now,
the audience
laughs as one,
like a dog's abrupt
once-over shake

## 25

so if we see this
*true scientific vision*,
is all then calm?
can we chill
like Lucretius said?

well, death still *devours*
and is called noisy,
the rapids' savage chatter,
and we, all of us,
waiting and wailing

but to know
that the moon
is not in fact
in travail,
that the winter sun
is not day by day
the more distracted
and incapable,
but to see that yes,
it's short-winded
but not so far advanced,
and remission is likely,
does this lighten our step
and refresh us?

if we can see through –
then blessèd are we
– and I mean lucky now

for all that happens is this:
microscopic variations,
macroscopic effects:
the classification
of regularities
is what it's down to

thus the airborne bacofoil
(as it would become)
for Cockburn's
phantom fleet
departing Dover;
thus Bernal with all
that could be known
of wave-motion
off Colleville-sur-Mer,
already in his pocket
grinds ashore
and is gathering samples
*re* tank-tracks
by D-Day + 1
(or so he claimed,
Solly, later Lord Zuckerman,
pooh-poohed it –
so was he there
or wasn't he?);
thus the penicillin moulds
for the dressing-stations;
thus the burn-rates
of wallpaper;
thus the war won,
thus Science and Society,
it all adds up,
sand tide and air,
rates and percentages
everything connects,
and here's Professor Leakey on
*God's inordinate fondness*
*for beetles,*
their giant success,

and the dangers
for shirt-fronts
of eating mangoes,
hence the logical
advice to eat them
in the bath

# 27

*after Riccardo Reis*


to be so imperturbable
would be to be
something soughing –
alliteration again,
it stole up on me
again

but I am not
to be laughed at,
this is my little rage
for order,
balance,
I do not want
to fall off

a poem should be
a paean
to law and order –
what else is there?
justice?
a 'land of'?

'soughing' is always
as of the wind,
was when *swōgan*,
do not be perturbed,
there is always the wind,
button up your overcoat

to see the soul of Nature
in the forms of matter –

sounds heroic,
but is it best,
knowing how things are,
to be always about the house
interpreting?

the mechanism
does not need us for this,
there is nothing latent
requiring us,
we are free for now –

there, there, there
it is!

## 29

what means anything
is dispersed:

a badge or bones
stirred by a plough

the woods still seared
from when a man
drove in, parked
and set himself alight

## 30

what is not austere,
and what is not true,
and what is not stupid
to say,
is folded in your note,
to be found in the event,
in your special box,
which – paraphrased – says:
when you read this
I shall have gone
to be with your father again,
that is where I really
want to be

this is the kind of way
we look at death,
it is not – especially when
elaborated – austere,
and it is not true,
and it is not a stupid thing
to say

# 31

*the figure raising his arm*
*in the main boat*
*is possibly a self-portrait*

but why would he
be doing with that
when it is the deep
and the sky
that matters here?

*raising his arm*
can barely be seen –
is he awaiting
a detail of the painting?
even then how much description
would he need
to be himself?
more than a belt, a hat
and a shirt – in fact
there can never be enough
which is why I don't believe it –
look, catch sight of me! no

sadly, perhaps,
he has given up his ghost
to the deep and the sky
and to what light does to him,
if not yet renounced
what the composition
requires,
which could be
a raised arm

*real*, not mum
's the word that taunts us
since there's no end to it
and no end of it
for the world –
to say no more –
is very full
and no one can tie it,
like a cord of hickory or stone,
and carry it home,
or even, if they are honest,
say this or that will do
to stand in for it
tempting as it is
to start figuring
with this cicada,
at sea on a clean shirt,
as I use a straw
to lead him
at least as far as
the washing-line
(the kinder philosophers
are said to set down
their caterpillars)

O blessèd thing,
save yourself!
O world!

still trying
to catch a glimpse

*real* though will do better
than most words
to humiliate –
all those worlds
I, you, he, she
do not live in:
the coalmines
of cake and milk,
the steel bowls of truth
at which we scrub and scrub
and never see ourselves

## 34

the stone will not
remember for us,
we have to perform the office:

enter the miserable
grammatical dream
where Cain says:
*there is no judgement*
*and no judge and no other world;*
*therefore there is no good reward*
*to be given to the righteous,*
*and no punishment*
*for the wicked,*
and in the hollowing of the stone
drives a stone
into his brother's brow
and slays him again
and again

knowing that everything is
just fretwork
should free us
from all that,
except we should not be
freed

## 35

our word for today
is *system*

Dad liked systems
of his own devising
such as those
for the filing of guarantees,
the storage of plant-pots and raffia,
booking the south coast
Allocation Train,
the Allo-cation Train

all this seeks and defends:
go on spec and you could be
out on the street
at 7 in the morning
and what we want
is all the three of us together
with a song in our heart
along the prom prom prom
tiddly-om-pom-pom
and everything going
according to plan

could he have thought
of himself as *system*
in the sense of whole,
everything for the use of
added up
divided with no remainder
a place for everything
like ashes and compost
and salvage?

no, he could not,
could not keep his hair on,
and who can?
he knew that what ought to be
is not, and though
systems of shoeboxes
and pastille tins
did help the three of us
live together –
do not disrespect
such things' place
in harmony –
they are defiance only,
and longing:
let the world
be settled up like this

*some hopes*
was a favourite phrase he had,
some hopes I still like to have

# 37

*sometimes … one can glimpse –*
like the rising
or setting sun
will catch a window
twenty miles away,
toy with it,
have it dance and blaze
in rapture
or immolation
until the angle shifts
and again it is
workaday glass?

we know how we saw this,
and how it happens,
but what it was
in the sense of
substance,
something you could cup
your hand around
like other flashing lights
on tractors or road-works,
is something else again

'Goggles', the painter,
'Speccy-four-eyes',
painting himself to look out
of the mirror
as though it is a witness-box,
alleges that that's the way it is:
the world does not front up,
plant itself
like a bouncer in a suit,
and give us time
for our assizes


look! something else like it
again, a little sashay
on the kitchen floor

and gone

like a cat over a wall
like a lizard past a stone

# 38   Epilogue

*For* [my emphasis] *thee*
*the world of fragrant flowers is drest,*
*For thee*
*the Ocean smiles and smoothes his wavy breast*
*and Heav'n itself*
*with more serene and purer light is blest*

and, as well:

*How EXQUISITELY the individual Mind*
*(And the Progressive Powers no less of the whole SPECIES)*
*To the external world is FITTED.*
*AND how EXQUISITELY too*
*the external world*
*Is FITTED to the Mind.*

> – Did you hear?
> – What?
> – That
> – What?
> – *The sunbeam said, 'Be happy.'*
> – Really?
> – *It loves us now, this Vale, so beautiful,*
>    *Begins to love us!*

Now read on:

## 39

there is an abyss of words
approaching
but no notice:

how can an abyss
approach?
I do not know,
I am not responsible
for the exact phrasing
only the re-use
but the ground
is softening
becoming spongy
elastic, springy

O world!

now read on

# call death an observation

i

call death an observation,
a supplied fact, ever more precisely noted,
(though mistakes have been made, ask any Goth)
and some vital sign may still be missed –
a monitoring may be merely mechanical,
conducted dozily after lunch, or not adhere
to best practice –
but from the many instances
the law 'We Die' has been induced,
and if shaggy at first, improvised –
and may still be so compared with
what might be to come – is now deduced,
the maths showing us how much we can infer
of what we do not know

it seems irrefragable, and as long as the law
coincides with observation it holds

## ii

if lines and circles are all our own work
have we invented death?
motionlessness seems to be
what was decided upon,
that she or he could no longer shift for herself
and would just dry there
or deliquesce depending,
although many (most?)
have traditionally not gone on such appearances
but when forced to give up say:
but this is not the real line,
what is real has no lines
because no space or time
because a line must be an act in time
and mind

because it is not bearable
to live with lines and circles

## iii

mathematics makes up the bolus,
what could be truer than such proceedings?
the equations of fluids in and fluids out,
the charting and cross-checking
towards a line to be pronounced upon:
the baby-like milky regurge
at the corner of the mouth,
sent out, uncalibrated, bubbling slightly

but somewhere there the point –

it happens always and the line is true

\*


and before the May-dawn, the conventional dream-ship,
bulk cargo freighter, or sharp-prowed liner,
the black *Normandie* or another such,
seemingly unworked, eyeless, unhurried;
and knowing you cannot row aside

# Acknowledgements

Special thanks to Judith Wainwright and Jon Glover, to my patient publisher Michael Schmidt, Judith Willson and all at Carcanet. Thanks too to a group of MA students from Manchester Metropolitan University for their comments on '... *and with the Indian figures 987654321 and zephira* ...'.

Some of these poems have appeared in *Cincinnati Review*, *Moving Worlds*, *PN Review*, *Stand*, and *The Reader*.

# Notes

The following notes acknowledge the sources of direct and adapted quotations that appear in the poems or their titles.

p. 7   Epigraphs: Ludwig Wittgenstein, from a letter to Bertrand Russell, 1913. Mark Rothko, 1949, quoted in James E.B. Breslin, *Mark Rothko, A Biography*, 1993.

p. 12   *we may be able to reduce the number of different things*: Richard P. Feynman, *Six Easy Pieces, The Fundamentals of Physics Explained,* 1998.

p. 17   *the visible universe can only be of the kind that permits us*: John D. Barrow, *The Origin of the Universe*, London, 1994.

p. 18   *the starting state of the universe must have been very highly ordered*: Barrow, as above.

p. 00   *the universe is like a pool that has had a stone thrown into it*: Attributed to Origen (*c.*185–*c.*254).

p. 20   *all the ordered forms of energy in the universe* ... : Barrow, as above.

p. 22   *there may be symmetrical universes but they are not ours*: Ian Stewart, *Nature's Numbers, Discovering Order and Pattern in the Universe*, 1995.

p. 25   *musicians wrestle everywhere*: after Emily Dickinson.

p. 30   **'against those who refuse definitions'**: see Aristotle, *Metaphysics*, Book IV, 4.

p. 00   *what need we know of the workings of Nature* ... : Roger Penrose, *The Emperor's New Mind, Concerning Computers, Minds, and the Laws of Physics*, 1990.

p. 32   *faith in reason is the trust that* ... : A.N. Whitehead, *Science and the Modern World*, 1925.

p. 34 ... *and with the Indian figures 987654321 and zephira* ...: see George Ifrah, *The Universal History of Numbers from Prehistory to the Invention of the Computer*, trans. Bellos, Harding, Wood and Monk, 1998.

p. 36 *a real sum is a sum of real people*: after the title of a photo sequence by Mario Merz.

p. 37 *the wall that separates* ...: from José Saramago, *The Year of the Death of Ricardo Reis*, trans. Giovanni Pontiero, 1991.

*'Mere Bagatelle'*

p. 39 *Epigraph: ... sometimes out of the corner of an eye...* : Jerry Fodor on Richard Dawkins, *London Review of Books*, 18 April 1996.

p. 50 10. *set yourself steadily...* : John Ruskin, *The Elements of Drawing*, 1857.

p. 55 14. *vast Rondures*: after Walt Whitman, 'Passage to India', Chant V, 1871.

p. 56 15. *of cousinhood or uncleship* – and *for a brief while*: after Charles Lamb, 'The Wedding', *Elia and The Last Essays of Elia*, 1835.

p. 59 18. *vous avez perdu l'homme il faudra le retrouver ce ne sera pas facile*: Victor Serge, *Les années sans pardon*, 1971.

p. 67 26. *God's inordinate fondness for beetles:* A 'quip' attributed to the biologist J.B.S. Haldane.

p. 73 31. *the figure raising his arm in the main boat...* : after James Hamilton on J.M.W. Turner's *'Now for the Painter'* in *Turner, The Late Seascapes*, 2003.

p. 76 34. *Cain says: there is no judgement and no judge...* : *Targum Pseudo-Jonathan* to *Genesis*, 4, 1–8 quoted in *The Oxford Bible Commenatary*, 2001.

p. 81 38. *For thee...* : After John Dryden, 'Lucretius, The beginning of the First Book', 1685.

*How EXQUISITELY...* : after William Wordsworth, 'Prospectus' to *The Excursion*, 1814.

*The sunbeam said, 'Be happy.'*: Wordsworth, *The Recluse*, Part First, Book First, 1806.